Sea Life
color by numbers

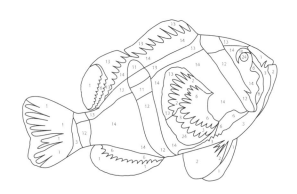

Sea Life
color by numbers

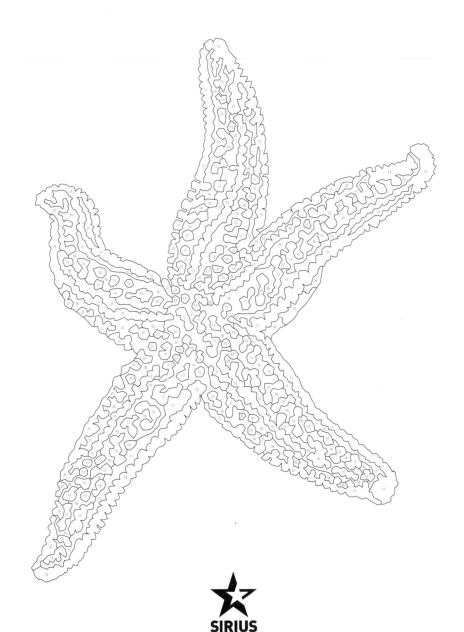

SIRIUS

SIRIUS

This edition published in 2024 by Sirius Publishing, a division of
Arcturus Publishing Limited,
26/27 Bickels Yard, 151–153 Bermondsey Street,
London SE1 3HA

ISBN: 978-1-3988-3629-7
CH011383NT
Supplier 29, Date 0424, Print run 5948

Printed in China

Introduction

The world's vast oceans and other bodies of salt water are home to an amazing variety of creatures and provide an inexhaustible source of beauty and inspiration. From little fish meandering around coral reefs to great ocean predators erupting from the waves, these pages will fill you with hours of delight.

The vibrant scenes of coral reefs, exotic fish, majestic whales, and other charming sea creatures will be a tonic to anyone seeking to escape their everyday life for a short while. Each image holds a promise of fulfilling hours of peace and pleasure, no matter what creature you choose.

Each marine artwork is fully numbered so that, by matching your pencils to the color key, you can gradually create a lovely sea life scene. If there is no number that means the space should be left white or colored with a white pencil.

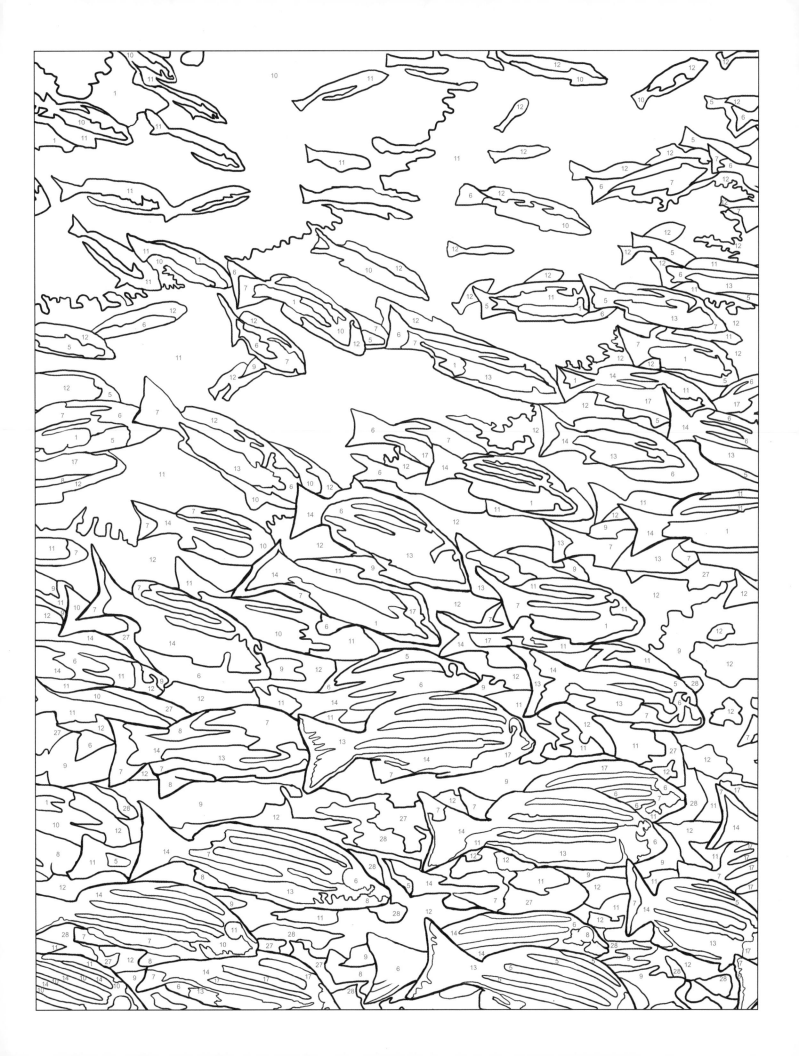

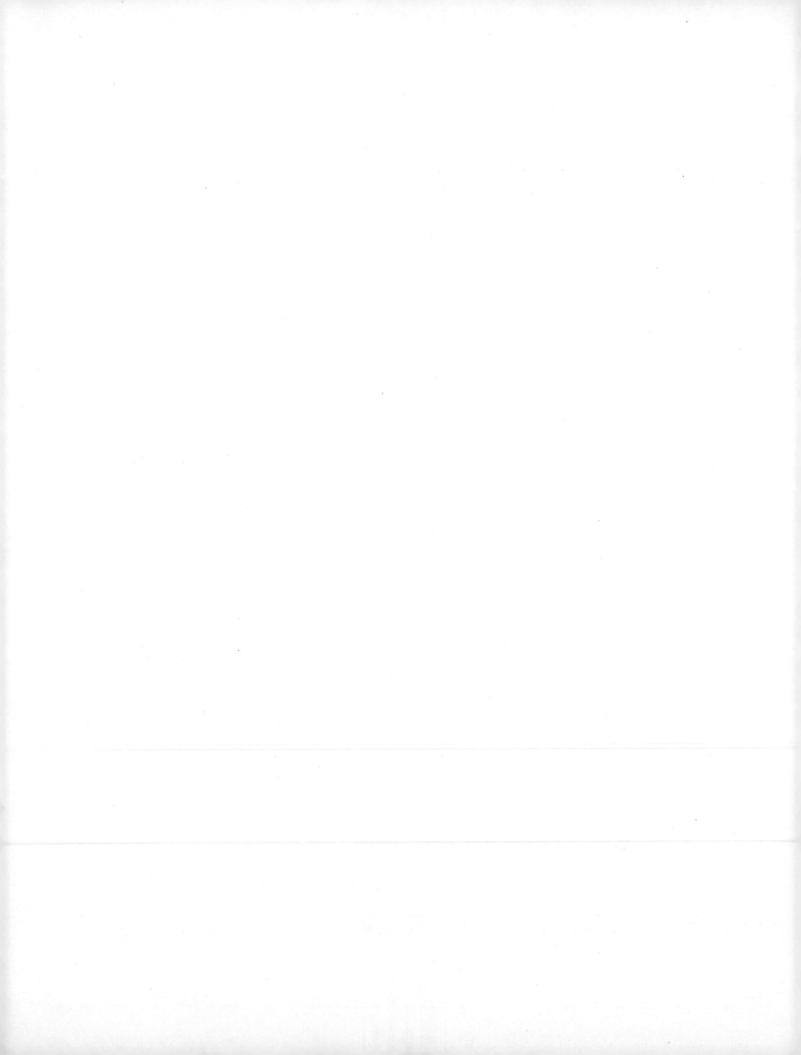

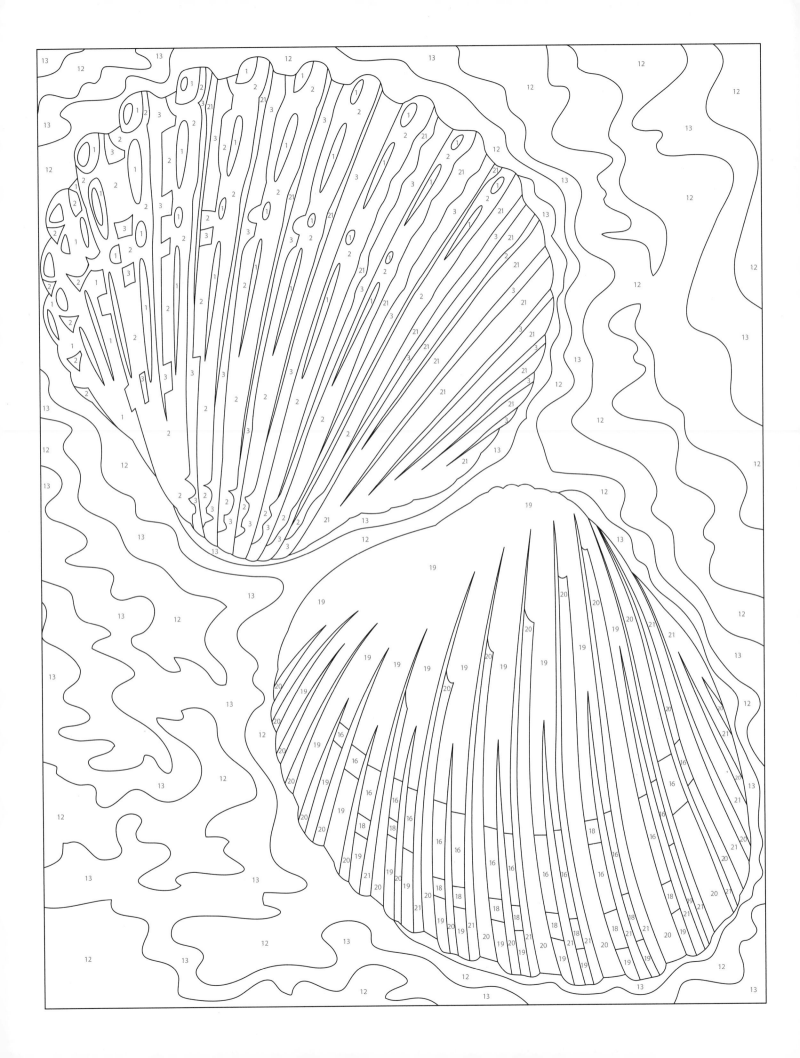

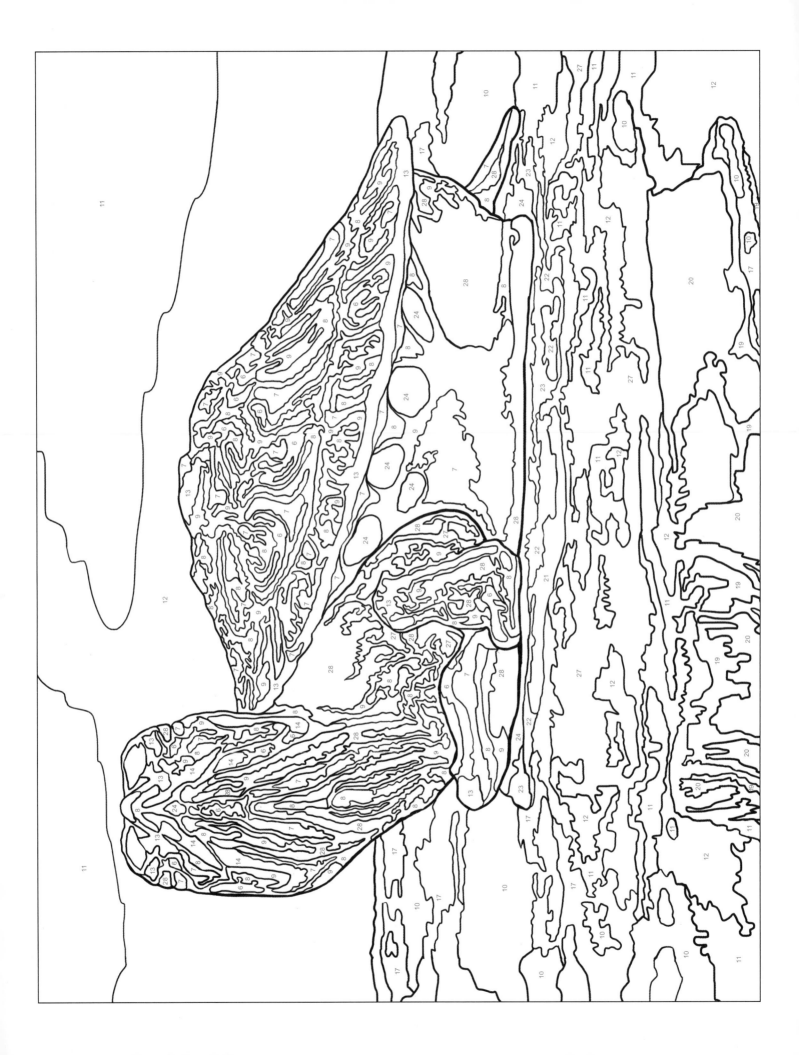

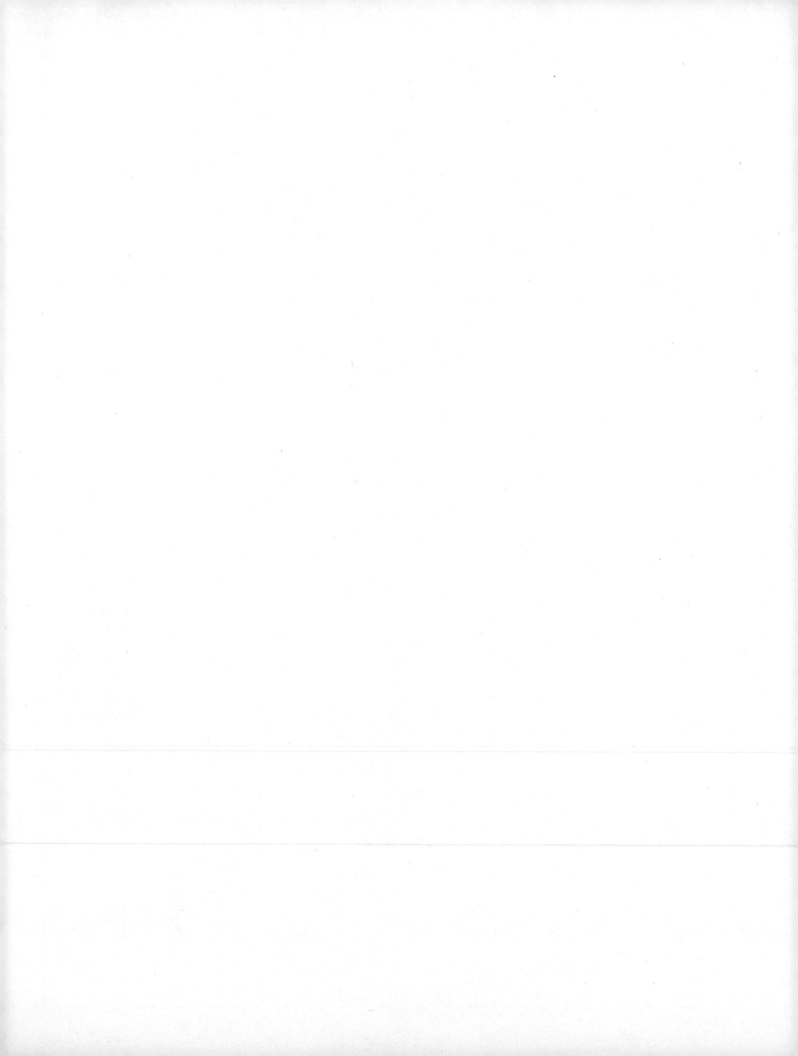

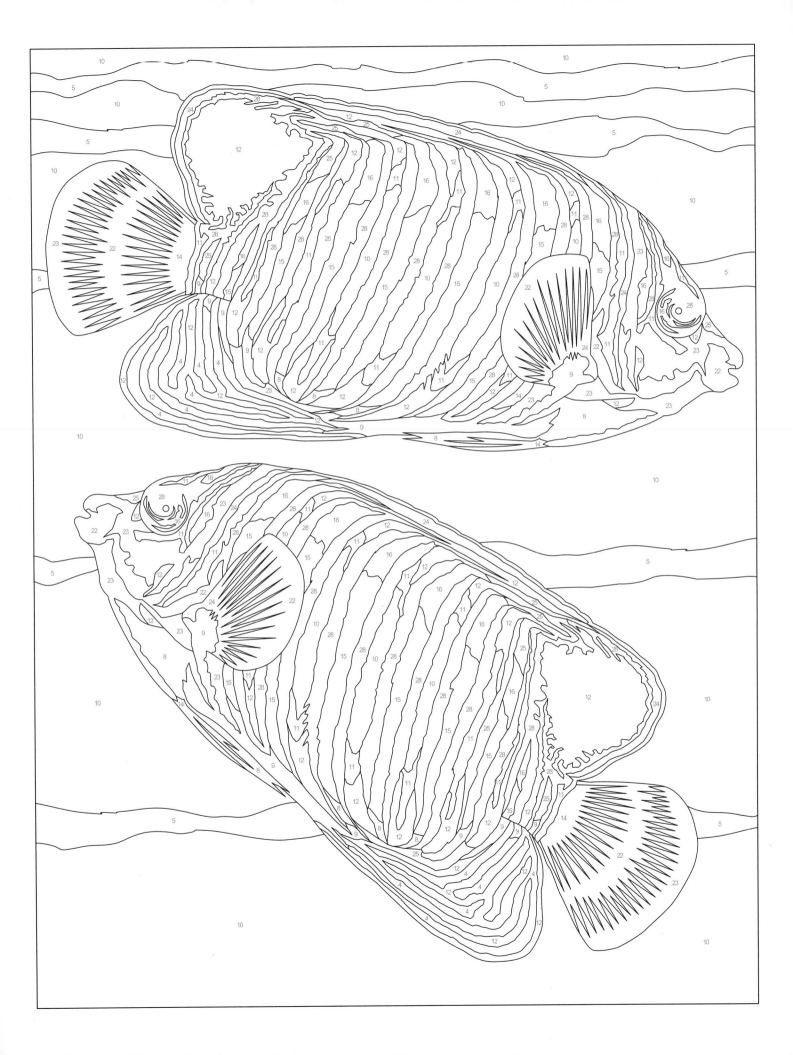

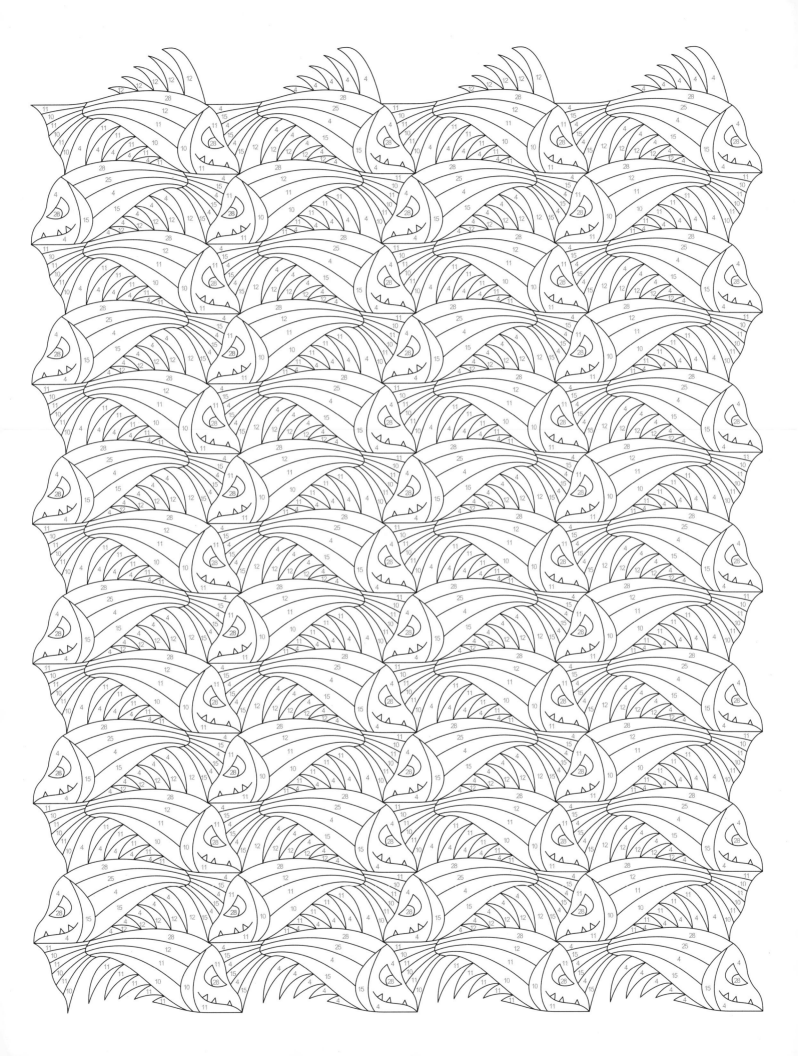

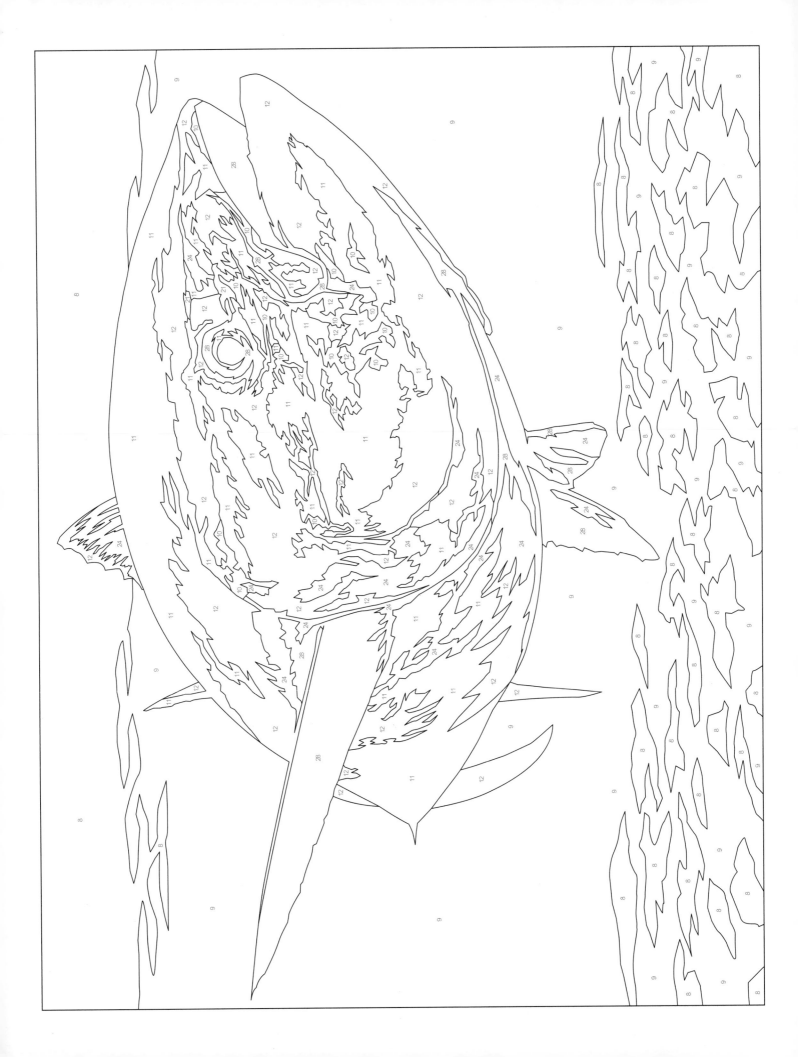

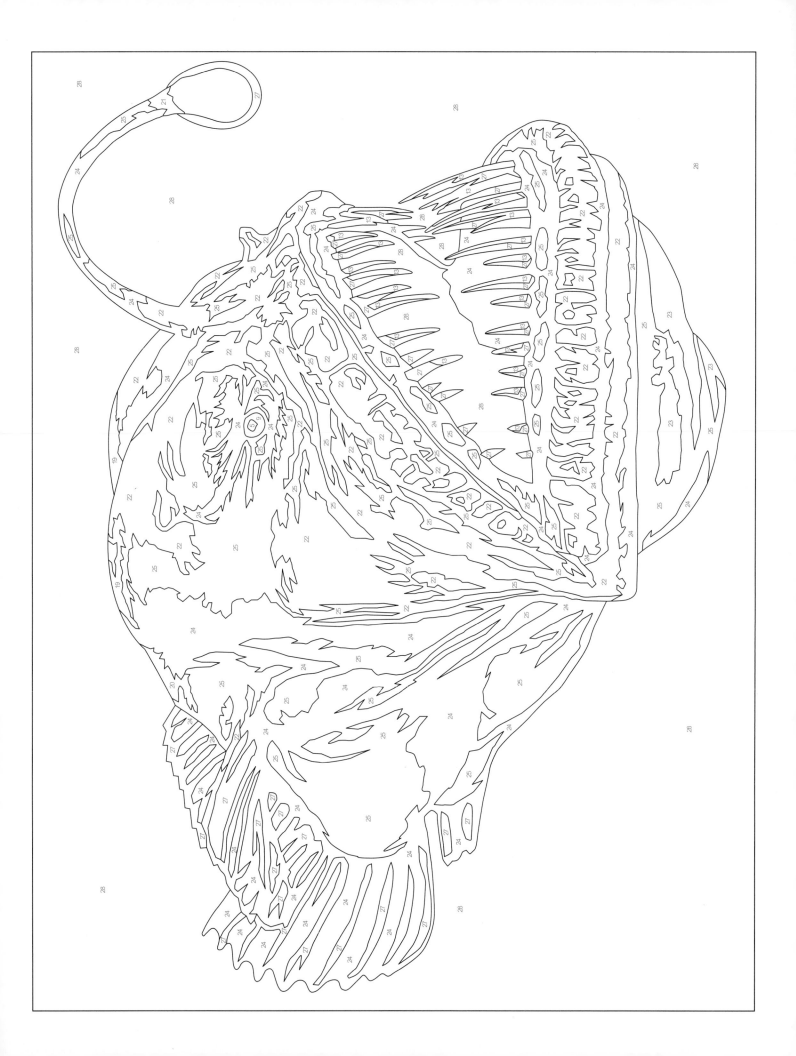

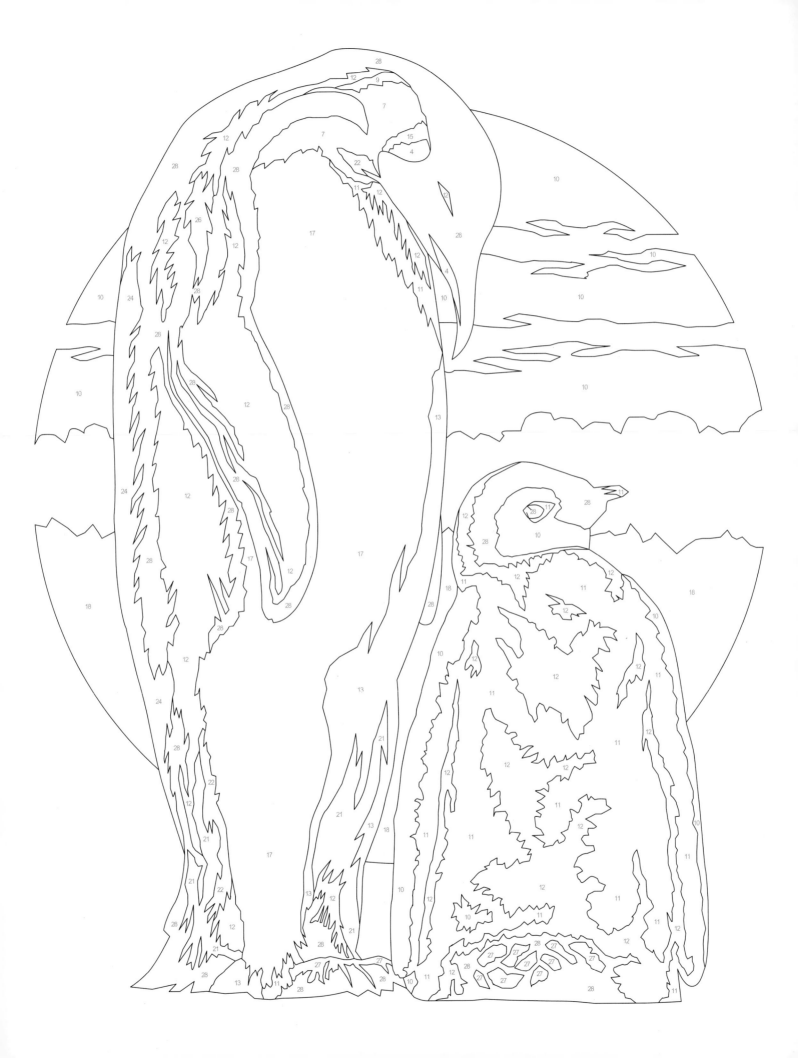

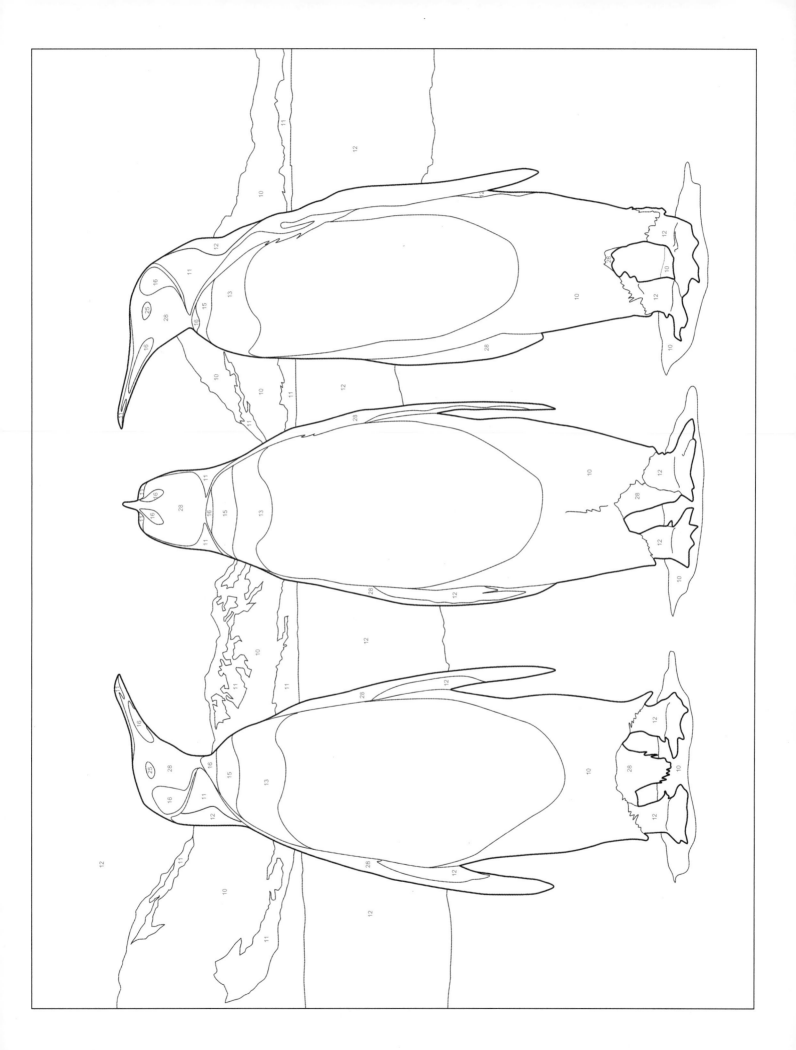

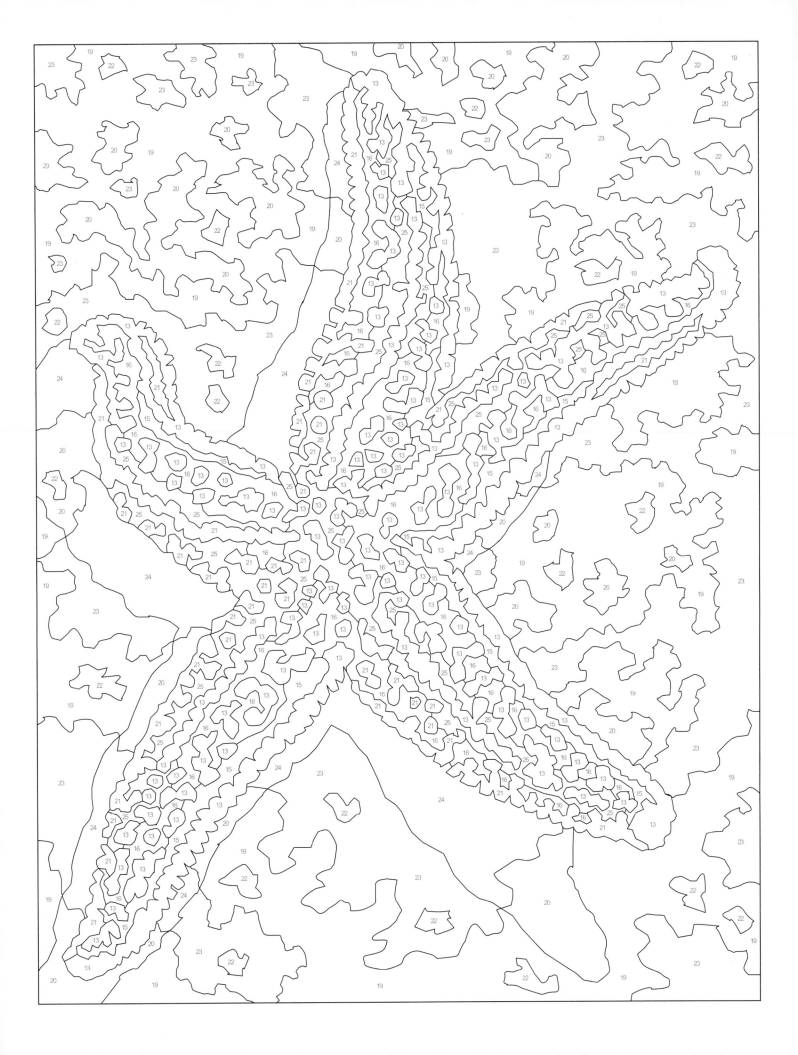

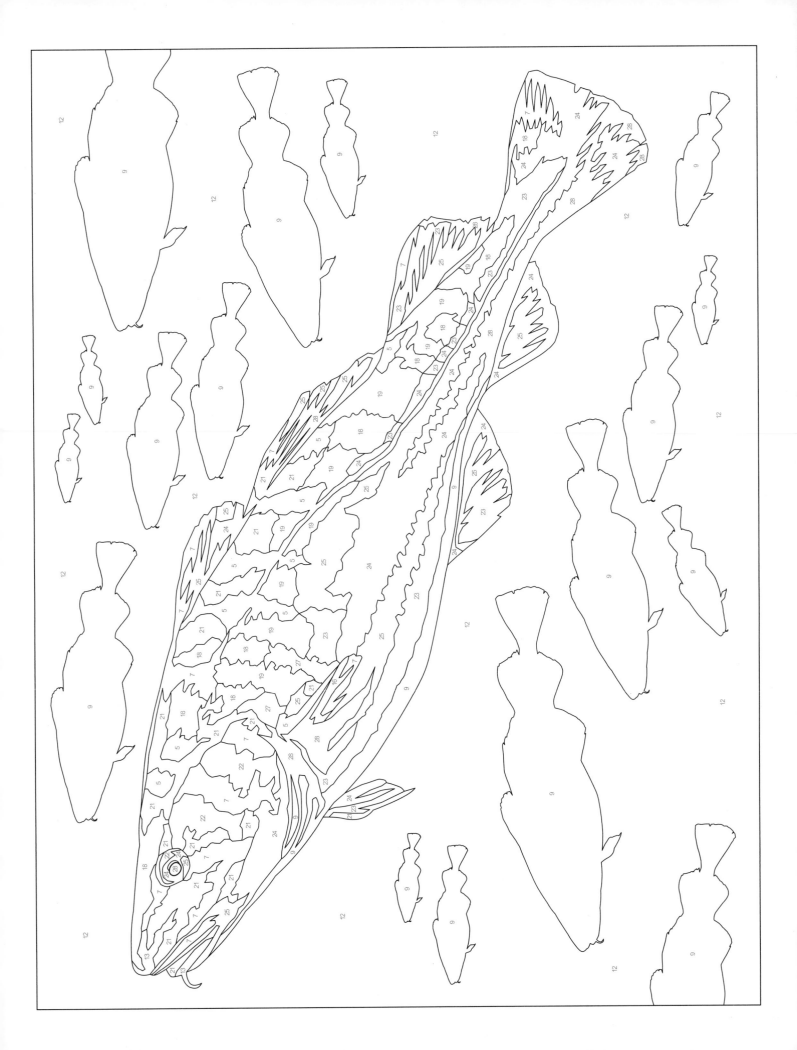